DICHTEN =
No. 17

No. 1: Friederike Mayröcker, *Heiligenanstalt*, 1994
No. 2: Elke Erb, *Mountains in Berlin*, 1995
No. 3: Ilma Rakusa, *Steppe*, 1997
No. 4: Ernst Jandl, *reft and light*, 2000
No. 5: Oskar Pastior, *Many Glove Compartments*, 2001
No. 6: Ludwig Harig, *The Trip to Bordeaux*, 2003
No. 7: Gerhard Rühm, *i my feet*, 2004
No. 8: Gerhard Roth, *The Will to Sickness*, 2006
No. 9: Ulf Stolterfoht, *Lingos I-IX*, 2007
No. 10: *16 New (to American Readers) Poets*: Ann Cotten, Franz Josef Czernin, Michael Donhauser, Ute Eisinger, Daniel Falb, Hendrik Jackson, Margret Kreidl, Bert Papenfuss, Steffen Popp, Monika Rinck, Farhad Showghi, Hans Thill, Raphael Urweider, Anja Utler, Ron Winkler, Uljana Wolf, 2008
No. 11: Peter Waterhouse, *Language Death Night Outside*, 2009
No. 12: Anja Utler, *engulf — enkindle*, 2010
No. 13: Monika Rinck, *to refrain from embracing*, 2011
No. 14: Elfriede Czurda, *Almost 1 Book / Almost 1 Life*, 2012
No. 15: Farhad Showghi, *End of the City Map*, 2014
No. 16: Michael Donhauser, *Of Things*, 2016

Elke Erb

The Up and Down of Feet
Poems 1994-2010

selected & translated from the German
by Rosmarie Waldrop

Burning Deck/Anyart, Providence

DICHTEN = is a (not quite) annual of current German writing in English translation. Most issues are given to the work of a single author. Editor: Rosmarie Waldrop.

Individual copies: $14
Subscription for 2 issues: $24

Distributor:
Small Press Distribution, 1341 Seventh St., Berkeley, CA 94710
1-800/869-7553; www.spdbooks.org

Some of the translations were first printed in the magazines *Aufgabe, Chicago Review, Colorado Review, Drunken Boat, How2, Verse,* and the anthology *After Brecht,* ed. Karen Leeder, Manchester: Carcanet Press, 2006.

Burning Deck is the literature program of Anyart: Contemporary Arts Center, a tax-exempt (501c3), non-profit corporation.

Cover image: "Three Figures in Context:" Selectively Fogged & Toned Monoprint by Denny Moers, 1987 (Egypt). Courtesy of the artist.

© 1994 by Steidl Verlag
@ 1998, 2000, 2005, 2007, 2010 by Urs Engeler Editor
Translation © 2017 by Rosmarie Waldrop

ISSN 1077-4203
ISBN 978-1-936194-23-0

CONTENTS

Prelude: My Letterature ... 7
I from *Unschuld, du Licht meiner Augen*, 1994 ... 9
   Archive (9/10/92) ... 11
   Getting Wind of a Plan (10/2 Berlin-11/7/92 St.Médard) ... 12
   But the Question Is (12/22/91) ... 13
   Sunflowers Are No Longer Sunflowers (2/3/93) ... 14
   Taken In (August 93) ... 15
II from *Mensch sein, nicht*, 1998 ... 17
   A Sign from Elsewhere (2/28/94) ... 19
   Talking to Oneself Is Just a Roar from the Sea (May-7/3/94) ... 20
   The Feeling of Profit (6/20/94) ... 21
   Train Across the Spree River (9/20/94) ... 22
   To be Human, Not: (10/23/94) ... 23
   Train Window (1/2/95) ... 24
   E.F., Emigrant (1/6/95) ... 25
   Now I've visited the Etruscans (2/6/95) ... 26
   Miraculi Mundi (2/19/95) ... 27
   So Very Jesus (3/8/95) ... 28
   Horse (7/16/95) ... 29
   A Dictionary Is (7/20/95) ... 30
   Hello Jürgen Becker (8/3/95) ... 31
   The Smile Pitiful (8/12/95) ... 32
   A Rhyme on Ever (8/29/95) ... 33
   Mindaugas Won't Survive Long (3/10/96) ... 34
   Appearance (6/30/96) ... 35
III from *Sachverstand*, 2000 ... 37
   Declaration (6/27/97) ... 39
   Of Course, Slowpokes Can Also (July 98) ... 40
   To Translate, the Road Blinking (8/5/98) ... 42
   Raw Material, Virgin (8/19/98) ... 43
   Attempt in Words (8/23/98) ... 44
   Meaning (she means... (10/9/98) ... 45
   Hölderlin, When I Was Young? (11/1/98) ... 46
   Be That as it May (11/20/98) ... 47
   Deterrent (12/21/98) ... 48

Different as Hansin and Erwin (4/3/99)	49
Russia as it Moved On (6/30/99)	50
"Back from the War" (7/18/99)	51
IV from *Gänsesommer,* 2005	53
Harried (2000)	55
The Up and Down of Feet — Horace (7/24/01)	56
As a Member (2/1/97)	57
Exactly (9/1/01)	58
Goose Summer (1/19/03)	59
V from *Sonanz,* 2007	61
Amusement (4/18/03)	63
The Two of Us (9/20/03)	64
Hens & Hills (10/1/03)	65
Erotic Combination (10/6/03)	66
Transitory (11/7-8/03)	67
Association (11/12/03)	68
Upright (1/8/04)	69
From Holland to Spain (1/29/04)	70
Incomprehensible — Donkey — Goat (3/30/04)	71
The Sky Rural (6/7/04)	73
Meditation (10/26/04)	74
As firm as (2/6/05)	75
Penny Dreadfuls (2/8/05)	76
Seen from Above (3/10/05)	77
That One (3/21/05)	78
A Tame Subjunctive (5/18/05)	79
For Instance (5/24/05)	80
Investigation (7/5/05)	81
Warning (7/8/05)	82
VI from *Meins,* 2010	83
Inconspicuous (11/28/03)	85
Remembered (7/6/03)	86
All Too Rarely Do We Understand Something (10/7/03)	88
Childhood (2/4/05)	90
Us Faces (10/6/06)	91
Theme (12/20/07)	92
Morning dawns... (4/20/08)	93
Bionote	95

MY LETTERATURE

Ah, Abraham-A, ah, nurse's breast-B,
O lala! C-major-C, daring-D, rotten egg-E,
farcical-F and gag-G, hushbaby
blue-hills-H, my inconceivable-I,
all sorts of jolly-J, kangaroo-K, lazy lice-L!
And you, Urmother-M, Urmother-M, you
and my saber of a nose, my chin-N,
Olala-O, too, and you, palm-P,
you, question-Q with a rolled-R,
ah, and silver-S, tinpan-alley-T, utterly uvular-U,
vernacular-V and weltschmerz-W, then ex-X,
xylophon-Y and cyclops-Y on the way to zero-Z
and Abraham-A, ah, nurse's breast-B,
ah, my coucou cousins and
bodily bugles and winds,
who, I ask you, can find
the heart to put you out of mind?

I

UNSCHULD, DU LICHT MEINER AUGEN
[Innocence, light of my eyes]

ARCHIVE

Closer than to the secret service files am I, I'm sure, to my own memory.

Even when it fails completely.

GETTING WIND OF A PLAN

How can anyone be rain and wind,
that is falling and blowing, and a path on a rock ridge
and rose hip and iron maw
and wings in clear air
and choking on it all at the same time?

for Friederike Mayröcker

BUT THE QUESTION IS

When I thought — back then, oh how slow to
pay attention in the closed circle! —

that the second house in a row of absolutely identical
houses was already no longer the same (let alone

identical), WHAT ELSE COULD
I HAVE HAD IN MIND? I can't imagine.

SUNFLOWERS ARE NO LONGER SUNFLOWERS

To snuff out,
like flames, all feelings

as if they should
like everlasting hell

as if vanished
into thin air

TAKEN IN

Monstrous that a person
could in a stretch of brook, with alders,
a bank lined with alders, with a meadow
— and a small gray cattle bridge jolt —

where there reigns
such constant and close
quiet,

that a person could there

be reflected, yes, mirrored, so,
as you look, it goes right through your soul
without resistance — this or that!
No cat would be taken in!

II

MENSCH SEIN, NICHT
GEDICHTE UND ANDERE TAGEBUCHNOTIZEN

[To be human, not
poems and other journal entries]

A SIGN FROM ELSEWHERE

My imaginary mother
from time to time utters a high note
a sign
of replete life.

But it's deceptive she is
no longer she is

a soprano since she emigrated.

(with greetings to Franz Hodjak)

TALKING TO ONESELF IS JUST A ROAR FROM THE SEA

because the self, as we've got it,
the pure
— in the blink of God's jealous and sanctimonious eye —
gold

that our Klondike claws, Siberian, Carpathian,
scraped from rugged quartz:

extraordinarily soft
and elastic, easy

to modify mechanically, and
slow to react,

a monstrance disk it nods on its stem,

neither listens nor talks itself,

an essence
of our innermost brain —
O blastula, O gastrula, O guest

from distant seas, come
as itan essence
of were with rising ponds,

an amoeba, in
pond's ear a roar from the sea.

THE FEELING OF PROFIT WHEN THINKING THAT POEMS CARRY KNOWLEDGE

quicker-than-a-wink wide-spread interest comes swimming
shoulder-high, surrounds you like a pond,
as if it meant to find out what's what,
and certainly existed.

From this deceptive height the eye drops
to elbow level: business tips.

Now wave-green over it all, water
whacking the quay.

TRAIN ACROSS THE SPREE RIVER

Yes it strokes
me, soothing

below, from quay to quay the precise strokes,
lead grey, pleasingly precise ripples,
the water. — It is

at one with itself as well as
everything else as well as

in motion, engaged in continuous
adjustment, as everything is, except

in concepts there's rest.

If only we'd sensed,
O you all five of my senses,
this in time!

Now I don't suppose we'll get,
O you my poor orphans,
another chance.

TO BE HUMAN, NOT:

a horse that rears — and bolts,
its head a trace,

reins like tangled trajectories
slung all through the body.

TRAIN WINDOW

In the sun in front of his house
between mountain face and railroad

an apple tree
he trims, on a ladder.

Must have heard the bells toll that
we don't live forever.

E. F., EMIGRANT

Once clear of danger he
wanted to know, what did it consist in?

Its name: not you.

Figures of speech, mechanisms,
carvings without knife or norm.

Like lettering
a traveler
could read.

* * *

Now I've visited the Etruscans.

Like that earlier time, in the giant Washington museum (with the golden Indian on horseback outside), before the glass case of "Pre-Columbian Art:" This was enough; why again? Why — start all over again?*

I walk from case to case — a rather casual presentation, as if the loot thieved from the tombs had been installed with some embarrassment: What's done is done, this is what we took. I walk from vase to vase and feel my eyes relax, grow easy, *cleansed by beauty.*

And: the word *ancient* — if you don't think (reflect) but look — has no meaning at all. Everything is new and shows: how it is made and intended, in all its elegance, a dance of what from the graves, utensils.

What's amazing: how come no kitsch? Like the stuff eagerly added to one altar or another in even the finest churches? (And whence the cave spirit of these ever more beautiful churches, caves in broad day? Surely not from underground?)

Sepulchral relics. Slaying, stabbing, hanging and strangling, torture, poison, drawing and quartering, illness, age. — Beauty, made to order.

---

*This question accepts the claim to perfection inherent in our concept of art. Aside from the fact that this claim usually (thanks to our society's unwise standards) appears as a distorted absolute, the aggressive point of the question "Why again?" conjures behind its own back the conditions of historical reality — and then has to shut up.

MIRACULI MUNDI

At the foot of the Berto (invented) a transparent pyramid
of layers of glass, layered to make it
unbreakable.

Inside, in spirits, pure as gold,
resembling an ear in some light,
the embryo of the, then, next in line ruler.

SO VERY JESUS

Below the mosaic dome of the apse a band of sheep,
rams, six on the left and six on the right.

From the one in the middle,
the runt, the odd one out,
the thirteenth —

as if shrunk
in a secret noose —

to those others: a charge of inner light such
that their backs seem to take wing.

Santa Maria in Trastevere, Rome, 3/8/95

HORSE

When sadness begins its ascending line:
the feel of a jolt, haste, flight impulse, anticipating
the chaos of hysteria germinating

in the wintery ground, its tiny green cropping up,
Where then, without horseman, do I gallop...?

A DICTIONARY IS

after all only
inferred from the sounding of sound-existence,
hence a rather approximate (somewhat, at times)
piano.

HELLO JÜRGEN BECKER

A buzzard-I, sailing, pulls together, overlaps views.
I follow. A palimpsest is neither composition nor lived.
I-projection, the buzzard flies in the "vertex,"
as we mathematicians called it when we still existed.

THE SMILE PITIFUL

how recast in words what upsets us
bird nailed to a black post

how escape words that don't protect
from all that bares its teeth behind our back

so that, in the coffin,
jutting out from the inevitably

rotting crumbling face
the teeth still make a lovely

smile.
Bird: as leaves molder — pulled upward.

A RHYME ON EVER

The bushes, the bushes, the brambles,
the clumps of wild roses and round sloes
have torn our gaze forever
into bushes, brambles, roses and sloes.

x

MINDAUGAS WON'T SURVIVE LONG

Unifies ca. 1240 a factious Lithuania,
won't survive long.

In 1253 becomes a Christian, is crowned by the Pope,
won't survive long.

In 1263 is murdered.
Again factions, relapse into paganism.

Brockhaus Encyclopedia

APPEARANCE

Stray dogs
are felt to be particularly close to reality.
But then they are gone again, vanished wittily
from the screen.

III

SACHVERSTAND

[Expertise]

DECLARATION

Do I perhaps carve fairy meat
and serve it on a platter?

And, in the unimpeded moonlight,
do fairy foxes

(that jump on the chairs round
the round table and rest their
forepaws next to knife and fork
on the white tablecloth)

perhaps sniff it before
the likes of me get to chew it?

OF COURSE, SLOWPOKES CAN ALSO

be quick, hit their stride,
you know all they ever do
is stir up!!
their dray ox fiber,

then when the solid body of thinking
and feeling, the stocky body of their
slowly formed opinion

takes wing I'd call it double-quick,
a quick flick, lickety-split,

no lack of buoyancy and
whiz, and carefulness doesn't
come close to describing their previous

inexorable pre-
paration, accumulation until
the need is ripe.

I mean they pay attention, account
for circumstances — their
spitting image, and

brook no contradiction
(don't even expect any).
True, the speed of slowpokes

in syntactic ambiguity, in any case,
is never as speedy as the speedies

who as it were have hardly
when — in a jiffy! — they're
gone again and while still

— x times — swiftly winging it
in such tiniest tittliest intervals like
mere particles of air — this too

is impressive!

TO TRANSLATE, THE ROAD BLINKING

Sleeping pack animals whose heads on the long road
down distances and years forget, instead of *whisper*
one might also say *sigh* — perhaps.

The road we covered, now emptied of us,
abandoned by all spirits, welcomes
a different desert called steady October

rain. Not that the treetops still
waved wavered swayed, camels in the
formerly yellow, nothing behind us, above, not a thing.

RAW MATERIAL, VIRGIN

...truly universal thinking that doesn't just expose
one's own bias and/or braces itself on tradition, subgroup culture,
hence also embracing (one's own)

no way, forget it:
The eye that looks out for itself has no time to —
hunger (hang out?). And grudgingly.

This leads (to bring in what's below
the chin) — leads me (assuming

I'd ask) to consider the optical arrangement

as non-random, to expect from the depth
of momentarily (while he sleeps) unused army boots:
words grassroot-true or heartwood-hearty...

ATTEMPT IN WORDS

— or that he, in the clearing, at the knee
of... and around us... or who... (witches?)
... hands me a cup of chickory,

milky beige. Leads too far afield. Colts-
foot. Not enough. A wood scene, simply. De-
forested, soft. Kneehigh, but someone's

back perhaps against —
towering — the stump — and his
hand

hands me chickory
ether fragrance clearing coltsfoot legtide —

* * *

*meaning (she means/says) basically the same thin*g. The untutored
orangutan-pup firmly closes his fingers on
the thumb of his mother's hand clamped
on a branch. A mere reflex

prevents his fall as in *like falling leaves, down the
bursting hill crashes the rock* (Hölderlin, "Vulkan").

HÖLDERLIN, WHEN I WAS YOUNG?

Look how massive the precautions/sandbags, theirs,
were everywhere — in spite of the lost war —
hulky, immovable

so that not even a germ
of the thought of —

in spite of the loud "No more war!"

For because of them — opposite —
sleep high as a column of air,
blinding, daunting, weighed down our lids...

BE THAT AS IT MAY

I can't stop wondering:
again I slide down into sleep
for a while, give in

to the — however familiar —
change of perspective around the three corners
that stack up the small-town

floors in a pale
insipid other-world light. Nevertheless:
I wonder.

DETERRENT

Idol on the door post, protects against
an amorphous mass of whining misery. Form is
an ultimatum, a pleasure
to keep company with.

DIFFERENT AS HANSIN AND ERWIN

When I reach my spot in the park and, getting off my bicycle, think: "Today the birches are luminous" (for they shine out from their surroundings)
    it is an attempt — no: my usual exercise — to fit into the just now "potentially present" puzzle-structure of language and: draw it up.
    The sentence "Today the birches are luminous," never mind that it's only the trunks that are luminous, would indicate competely different "findings" or "facts" *on another planet.*

RUSSIA AS IT MOVED ON

How in Russia you, I would have been…eliminated. No matter under which regime: so it moved on, the way it knew. Damage. Moving on has its reasons as does what persists. Within it, each case its own kind of ruin (its own alienation and nothingness).

"BACK FROM THE WAR"

When Dad was on leave, walked around, and the grass, where he walked, looked slightly different around him, in relation to him — I thought this is the way it is, took my bearings from a clock.

IV

GÄNSESOMMER

[Goose summer]

HARRIED

27 August 2000
Before my eyes an instrument is being set up that then is supposed to work, as I — in the upper back corner of my head — suspect. Mechanics in blue overalls, adults.

28 August
If this happens again it is possible that I'll be pleased, because I'm reasonable.

30 August
The child watching senses the part of displeasure involved.
He is old enough for that.

Nevertheless he is pleased with all the others, and with the instrument, that it's going to work.
Thus he too is already dying.

Moreover, he runs ahead of the process, turns round to see how far they've gotten, comes back and watches again.

It doesn't take long, *vita brevis*, but nevertheless too long, and there are chasms, nothing to hold on to…

THE UP AND DOWN OF FEET — HORACE

with all his amazing syntax — the rhythms
(how do they play with syllable length?)

full of an energy, as if just set on their feet.
Harried with constant footfall. The ground
underneath. Tracks, in each case.

The ear hears a
gallop. There was more of that in the city.
As much of that as in the city.

And came men overland. Even more so.
In step, trot, army.

Spatium. Spur. Whir of names.

for Ulrich Keicher

AS A MEMBER

So if your kind lives in packs
or — a technically richer system — family clans —

what comes right after the carp's
been fed in the pond?
Well, nothing, or?

Opiates.

Are monkeys stimulated
when a member of the pack is pleased?
Does it depress them if one is in pain?

Is pleased:
any achievement (spirited leap, lucky catch)
may upset the hierarchical order.

Is a challenge for both sides an opiate?
Do monkeys also fight just to fight?

Alright.
A certain syndrome has come together here
(have I gathered here), "meaning" sorted out

(so sorted = meaning)!

EXACTLY

If an exercise, in which I willingly *"admit fear,"* were used as proof of my inferiority…, my disgrace: wouldn't that just dot the i.

GOOSE SUMMER

Gossamer — summer-
threads, Indian
summer,

a fine web, weft, finest gauze
in coffins, in death,

that's how I encountered it in Emily Dickinson,
(The Dews drew quivering and chill —
For only Gossamer, my Gown —)*

and as with the ringing of a bell
there rose, grew, flew
information —

of something encompassing, past, remembered
from earlier times, not mine, but general

and before it began to rise in the silence
as if the bell tolled the whole earth and just
as the bell is hollow…

morning light, bedroom, mirror,
you stand before the mirror, triple-winged mirror
in the bedroom, dress in your best

---

*"Because I could not stop for Death—"

on the floor between bed and mirror
you stand in mirror emptiness —

or cherryblossom-white
on your sleep-warm body, the freshly washed
blouse, white…

I recognize the shiver, not mine,
as the delicate weave,

as shirt, blouse, vest
face outward seeing death,

I recognize it, dress or dew.
They had it colder then, wore more clothes,

hooked, buttoned — so the cold,
after its first little blast
on bare skin

rose with layer after layer — until swallowed
by clothes — and now, with death,
into the day —

It was colder
in the house, but the grain
was full; the sun traveled and moved,
the children, the kids, kidded, the grave
didn't bat an eye.

V

SONANZ

[Sonance]

AMUSEMENT

Pavillions. Park-pavillions. Mangy.
Park-pavillions coughed into parks.
Go catch the plague.

Skullcapped
park-pavillions.

Stern ferns.

Approach, from below, time of approach,
surely not ascension to heaven. Crocus?
Pavillion-bells:

On floorboards. Round. Raw. Dammed up
air.

Stern ferns.

Martyred
city park. Sand boxes little bridges.

Not a living soul. Coocoo.

THE TWO OF US

Evening with many leaves. Unaware of itself...
We walk. Walk, walk. Fagged

out. The leaves reflect. Quiet.
To no end. Whirling spiral. Fagged out.

The chessboard soggy, wet. Swelling.
No duty paid, never lie.

Here, in earlier strata, might have entered
a hunter, carrying a rabbit.

HENS & HILLS

As soon as an idea appears follow it and promptly
vanish with it into perspective promptly
become absorbed

Hens today out of context
behind the fence today hopelessly out of context
today in sheer scatter

Under the dull high blue the dull high dusty blue
giants, *Hünen,* today out of context
locked in their megalith graves

EROTIC COMBINATION

Beard hair, the beard of an imagined
goat, but who would know her?

Under the treetops, gray, weathered,
a left corner post, wooden hut, let's say her shed.

Goat lip silenced across teeth.
Visible, kneehigh, the corner

of the post kneels pale in the dim forest-soil-light
to satisfy grazing eyes.

Stars moreover
still twinkling...

TRANSITORY

The cause was what mattered. Now we're done with it.
The cause, too, done for. Undone. Fly hum.

Little tyke stomps up from the meadow,
socks sagging, glowing cheeks, fist
full of buttercups.

By much washing slackened, the elastic.
Black and white cow.

And the water down there, it's run toward its goal
for almost ever.

ASSOCIATION

A crow flew past the window,
the air, hot, turned a deeper blue.

Beyond a doubt the wings seemed to — bless,
in a flitting way, but still.

Down by the lake, the field,
As down as looking up, as taking is in all its breadth.

Sowing by hand used to be. With measured pace.
A perpetuum mobile to the end.

UPRIGHT

That the grass stands up on the lawn
even in winter, at dawn.

Skeleton tree sweeps up what little light.
From light, air, earth grows our earthly time.

Daily climbs the lark to measure the sky
in other seasons. What little light kisses our eyes,

converts the skeleton to tree.
As long as it's alive, the body will arise.

FROM HOLLAND TO SPAIN

You see yourself from a great distance when you read about Holland. You could be anybody. Whoever reads about Holland is there in spirit. Holland's eminence pushes it into the far distance. Its eminence is composite, one thing connected to another. Naval power, commercial power, sheep breeding, lense grinding. Going, however, from Holland to Spain is almost no sweat. Just that trifle, France. Even the Pyrenees are nothing. On the contrary: no sooner named than you've crossed them. In Spain you buy meat. In the inns you ask for a free bed, a pot and fire. They are too few, they don't cook for travelers. Everybody brings his own when traveling in Spain. The era is the Baroque. The moon is uninhabited. We are not unreasonable.

INCOMPREHENSIBLE (I)

Between gas stove and table *the thought*

> a lonely donkey at the edge of a field
> a distant — Bulgaria! — memory
> Apparently lonely donkey —

Between gas stove and table *the thought*
that we die —

> the donkey does belong to someone,
> it's hitched to a little cart, behind them
> a vast corn field, the plain —

the thought
that we die —
down a maelstrom – gone —,

> there's nothing else in the world.
> As long as I can see. As my train
> passes en route to the Black Sea —

Incomprehensible

that we die —
down a maelstrom – gone —,
drained, drawn.

between gas stove and table *the thought*

> a lonely donkey at the edge of a field

DONKEY (II)

Stands the donkey, light gone out of his eyes.
A gray stone, leaves this life, remains.

Beard of Abraham, a sign, above the field.
The wondrous sign in miniature: beard of the goat.

Goat, goat, train gone by, abandoned donkey.
Horizon parallel to edge of field.

GOAT (III)

and goat beard, puts front hooves
on the bucket rim. Thus raised up
looks over the fence. That animal.

THE SKY RURAL—

you pause when it is striking, remember.
While seeing it you remember: it.
With brief regret, as you walk on.

Its emptiness holds blinding light.
It knows you creature from within.

MEDITATION

I stop to catch hold of myself — hadn't I better walk on?
Things get changed and arranged. To catch up with myself. Pleasure
to think of the outside, the outside before my eyes. Tree tops.
How I would twitter were I a bird.
Since I really dislike nothing.

Am I really going? — Go and hold still,
interval, defenseless.

* * *

As firm as the cloud,

that dark one, hanging low
as if heavy:

no guarantee —

no counting on, nothing can I protect,
no one console,

should I
they'll die, suffer, should
I leave

and forget the cat,
the drawing.

PENNY DREADFULS

The 19th century was fearful because it moved into
what its respectable industrialists and busy
by-scrapers

had emptied out, i.e. robbed blind: the once normal,
in intact nature natural *density of definitions,*
appropriate conclusions

from areas so complex they represent vastness.
And there was dark.

SEEN FROM ABOVE

She walks slowly with a dog.
She walks slowly, pulled by the dog,
park paths, high trees, snow,
Academy of Music.

One walks slowly, pulled by a dog.
The whole morning long she pulls.

Below. The Academy
of Music, a yellow building.

It's snowing.

THAT ONE

behind the fence, the fatso,
bent double, carries a slab
under his arm, into his house.

His nose at least has a straight back.

This is no scene, the empty windows
are empty windows. Elderberry bush.

Moon of a distant farm yard.
A horseback forms a sine curve,
the I, an oscillation.

A TAME SUBJUNCTIVE

The tram doesn't come Doesn't stop Shuts the door
before you get a foot on the step.

Something is complicated, not uncomplicated.
If only it were uncomplicated you could... The heart

a cat in mid-leap Uneventful
from top to bottom the trunk of the alder.

No tram in sight
This should not be

All kinds of logic
With their back to you With knife and fork before them

Now and then a meeow A rattle
All ear you and surroundings.

FOR INSTANCE

the stag with an axe in his shoulder. Roams on,
look: hit in the future with an axe in his shoulder,

roams North, on toward a future May,
intact nevermore because of imagination.

Gutters in a row, the road. Then a steeple,
city wall tower, a little old lady looks out,

forgetmenot, no more moon, the stag's jawbone,
dictionary illustration, the expression frugality. Grief.

INVESTIGATION

I go to have fun
come to have fun
come to

rabbits rabbit, beavers beaver, kids
kid, orphanage, fun
funs,

ghosts ghost, masters master,
legs leg it under coattails, coats
coat

& umbrellas umbrella, goats
goat, but unseen the ways sight
sights

soups soup, sums
sum, right, what-
ever

is goes on.

WARNING

The world is full of fish hooks. Folk song, all together now. The world is full of folk songs. The valley is empty of antlers. I dream great gates. Sunny morning, dream gates grate.

Behind the house the fields a bare ribcage. Rising and falling with breath. Ribs.

VI

MEINS
[Mine]

INCONSPICUOUS

I wonder whether he'll come

The beauty of such structures
(that you experience for instance when, in a path,
you recognize the intention)

can perhaps not be found/felt
in your own language.

And even here, in the foreign tongue, only
if you escape the protective blindness of your own
(its conventions and purposes)

and intentionally, free of purpose, keep frequenting
the foreign one.

Otherwise, if you don't in this almost selfless manner
redeem selfishness,
nobody in you will see

the poetic-beautiful artefact-sculpture of a group like

I want to go.
I wanted to go.
I want you to go.
He's wanted by the police.

REMEMBERED

For years Lili Brik lived in fear of being arrested. She did not know that Stalin had personally struck her name from the list: Mayakovsky's wife we won't touch.

How does one look — out of one's fear —
at a life that could/can go on
— its course, recourse, flow?

Is it yours?

In your eyes, is it an *it*, a *this*
with the accent, the aspect, the accessories
of your own?

Doesn't
even the pronoun *it* show too much
composure?

(Haven't we learned to articulate
beyond murder?)

Does it then go on without a grammatical subject?
And not as if born?

Lives, breathes, endures; barely scrapes by you.

As it endures, is it for you what we guess we would
call durable security?

The Russians smiled when there was talk of survival.
[…]
If we were uncomfortable with the smile of those who got off with a scare, when this smile played around the mouth of former prisoners it felt totally sinister.

for Christa Wolf's eightieth birthday

Quotations in italics from Fritz Merau: *Mein Russisches Jahrhundert: eine Autobiographie,* Hamburg: Verlag Lutz Schulenburg, Nautilus Editions, 2002

ALL TOO RARELY DO WE UNDERSTAND SOMETHING

B is an intelligent, active, creative man.
If I don't start from my perspective, but that of a person like him —

who is already in the habit of
arranging his own conditions/suggestions/ideas

and certainly also channels the entrance (reception)
of others' statements

(if I give my brain this little push, pop)
(OK, OK?) if for once I don't start from myself

but from such an active type,
he will, I realize,

hope that women will tell him
what he cannot grasp under his own steam,

and even lead him past the cliffs to dry land —
or, on the contrary, out to the open sea

(always a risk: we run aground on others as on ourselves).

She, however, the gifted woman,
has her own latifundia, her scope and scape (nature), and
unbroken strength, a gifted woman's strength,

though subject to the random will-o-the-wisp
of (yes? yes?) expected commands —

then of course it can't work out
it can't work out for the two of them!

In spite of everything. Pity!

Author's note: B is Bertold Brecht whom I here see more positively than usual. She is Marie Luise Fleisser, who is a boon to German literature but did not have much happiness. I kept the names out of the text because I consider it exemplary.

CHILDHOOD

Three houses (with yards) and ours, I
come out from between the cows. Cow flops drying,
tree stumps. Mushroom patches.

Fall fog. Wire fences, boundary stones, the
structured world.

US FACES

The rider would have passed by.
And below, violets
by the wayside, on a dry stretch,
the end, maybe, of a slope down to the road.

The rider, for a fixed moment, would have looked toward us,
out of the painting, toward all of us, all of us faces,
and in the lower right the clump of violets been
under the left hoof about to come down.

We could only think that the violets
would never be the same once the rider
had passed, or however else time had
trickled on, decline, place, facts

in a flow left to itself.
Flow it is called, but we insert: Afterwards
they are no longer the same. This touched us.

Van Dyck. Study for an Equestrian Portrait. 1634/35.
The suggestions in the air, in the upper right:
a slightly less sketchy figure of Victory bearing a palm

we ignored, didn't take into account.
The barely visible violets, however,
touched us deeply.

THEME

Putter around: Then you are things. Prey.
Take care or your eye,
as you putter, will pop out.

Light of your eyes: lantern. Outside.
Good for the night. And passenger traffic.

Your duodenum — looping back, looping forth!
Controlled by the nerves? The nerve authority?

Nerves, nerves!
Are left to themselves.
In the light breeze a rustling like leaves.

* * *

Morning dawns at the balcony door. It was never
clear: did it come from the world or was
the world here?

Strange, the question has a village–contour:
construction — here, vastness: world.

But would not be asked in the country. Is
therefore a city question. In a city
the city is never the world.

At best a precaution.

BIONOTE

Elke Erb, one of the most noted German poets, grew up in the former German Democratic Republic and lives in Berlin. She has published more than twenty volumes of poetry. A selection in English from her first three books (*Gutachten*, 1976; *Der Faden der Geduld*, 1978, *Vexierbild*, 1983) is available from Burning Deck under the title *Mountains in Berlin*. After the books represented in the present volume, there have appeared *Das Hündle kam weiter auf drein* (2013), *Sonnenklar* (2015), and *Gedichte und Kommentare* (2016).
Beside poetry Elke Erb has published a book of essays, *Der wilde Forst, der tiefe Wald* (1995), and translations from the Russian (Tsvetaeva, Achmatova, Chlebnikov, etc.). Her many honors include, most recently, the Georg-Trakl- and the Ernst-Jandl-prizes (2012, 2013).

Rosmarie Waldrop has translated, from the German, Friederike Mayröcker, Oskar Pastior, Gerhard Rühm, Ulf Stolterfoht, and, from the French, Edmond Jabès, Emmanuel Hocquard, and Jacques Roubaud. Her most recent book of poetry is *Gap Gardening: Selected Poems* (New Directions, 2016).